GREAT ARTISTS COLLECTION

Five centuries of great art in full colour

SEURAT

with an essay by ROGER FRY
and a foreword by ANTHONY BLUNT

ENCYCLOPAEDIA BRITANNICA : LONDON

Volume eleven

COVER: Detail from 'Le Chahut' (Plate 43)

This edition published in 1971
by Encyclopaedia Britannica International Limited, London

ISBN 0 85229 086 1

Printed in Great Britain

FOREWORD

TO THE GENERATION that was growing up in the 1920's, when Roger Fry was at the height of his career, the most influential part of his writings was that series of speculative essays in which he set forth his aesthetic theories. These he had evolved to explain and to rationalize the deep admiration which had been aroused in him by the work of certain late nineteenth and early twentieth century French painters, to whom he gave the generic name of Post-Impressionists. He was a prophet who, having discovered an aspect of beauty to which most of his fellow-countrymen were blind, was determined to open their eyes to it and quite literally to convert them to his own convictions.

'Prophet' is the appropriate word to describe Fry, for, although he was himself a strong free-thinker, his Quaker ancestry had a powerful influence on his mode of thought and gave it a character which was not far from religious enthusiasm. This was most strikingly apparent in his lectures; his appearance, his voice, his whole manner produced a feeling of awe in his listeners; when he talked about an artist whom he loved, the scales literally fell from one's eyes; and when he was dealing with a form of art of which he disapproved, though one might disagree, the impression was equally strong: it was like listening to Jonah cursing the Ninevites.

Fry, however, was a scientist by training, not a philosopher, and, viewed from a distance of forty years, some of his theories seem less persuasive than they did at the time. This is perhaps an unimportant and certainly a temporary criticism; for, when they were put forward, the theories served their purpose – to break down traditional aesthetic beliefs which prevented us from understanding the Post-Impressionists – and in a century they will be valued as among the clearest and most honest statements of a doctrine that was vitally significant during the first quarter of the twentieth century.

Fry never pursued speculation for its own sake; his theories were produced as explanations for what he had seen and felt; and both his eyes and his sensibility were quite unusually perceptive. His knowledge of works of art and his range of appreciation were both vast. He had blind spots – a refusal to recognize the qualities of Greek art was probably the most serious – but at one period or another of his life he studied and enjoyed an astonishing number of works of art of the most diverse kinds. Starting on perfectly conventional lines with a highly scholarly

3

knowledge of Italian Renaissance painting and a respect for the giants of the seventeenth century – Rembrandt, Rubens, Velazquez and Poussin – he was among the first English critics to write with understanding of El Greco, of Italian baroque painting, of so-called Primitive art, whether African, South American or Oceanian, and in his last years his deepest love was probably for the art of China and Persia; but his name will always be linked with the 'discovery' of French late nineteenth-century painting. As he himself readily admitted, he was far from being first in the field; certain enlightened French collectors had realized the genius of Cézanne, Van Gogh and their contemporaries a generation before Fry came to know them; their works had begun to be collected in Central Europe and even in America; and some interest had been shown in them by isolated enthusiasts in this country. But the fact remains that it was Fry and his friends who fought the battle to get the Post-Impressionists recognized in England, and though the exhibitions of 1910 and 1912 may seem in retrospect peculiar in their selection and unbalanced in their emphasis, they, together with the missionary work with which Fry and his friends accompanied them, broke the ice and prepared the way for the real understanding of an art which at that time was viewed with hostility and ridicule by most English critics.

It is probably the essays, some short, some longer, which Fry wrote on individual Post-Impressionist painters that will give us today the best idea of his qualities as a critic. In these his power of observation, his absolute humility and integrity in front of a work of art, and his ability to dissect his emotions without destroying their intensity in the process appear to the full and pure speculation plays a minor part, though in every case Fry seeks to arrive at general truths from his observations on individual artists.

Curiously enough Fry came to appreciate and love Post-Impressionist painting not through seeing the works of those painters who were eventually to be his real gods – Cézanne and Seurat – but through Gauguin, whom he later slightly frowned on as a Romantic, and Van Gogh, whom he was eventually to define – and this, from Fry, was a form of condemnation – as 'more an illustrator than a plastic artist'. His book on Cézanne – perhaps his most completely mature analysis of any artist – did not appear till 1927, and the essay on Seurat, printed below, was written to celebrate the acquisition by the Tate Gallery of the *Baignade* in 1924. In these two works Fry was faced with artists whom he admired and loved without qualification, and who did not raise within him all those troubling questions of theory which, though they make fascinating reading as examples of a highly intelligent mind trying to arrive at a precise definition of the truth, can sometimes be provoking to the modern reader. With Cézanne and Seurat Fry was not worried by the conflict between illustration and formal perfection; both artists were masters of plastic composition, though, as he pointed out, one derived his formal harmonies from a minute and humble contemplation of nature, whereas the other imposed on nature a rigid and preconceived system. Both Cézanne and Seurat had an intellectual integrity that satisfied an essential longing in Fry, for, although in theory he strove to dissociate aesthetics from ethics, his writings both on artists and on individual works of art are full of judgments which show that at bottom the two ideas cannot be wholly separated.

Nowadays we should probably not take such a strictly 'abstract' attitude towards the art of Seurat as that taken by Fry in the following essay. It is true that Seurat produced some of the most perfectly satisfying formal designs since Piero della Francesca, and also that he evolved a highly self-conscious and intellectual method of execution, but it is also true – and this is a fact which Fry admits but of which he minimizes the importance – that his pictures represent in vivid form the life of the middle-classes of Paris and its suburbs in the 1880's. It would be foolish to read into his painting a social or political programme, but it cannot be a matter of chance that such a high proportion of his small early paintings represent subjects like stone-breakers or peasants at work in the fields. It is true that they are not treated with the violent compassion of a Van Gogh, or with the political consciousness of a Courbet, but they are equally far removed from the dispassionate curiosity with which Degas studied human beings in their various occupations; and it must not be forgotten that Seurat was a friend of Camille Pissarro, Félix Fénéon and others who were enthusiastic anarchists.

In Seurat's later works the problem is more complicated. The artist is certainly not putting forward any political or humanitarian thesis; on the other hand the *Baignade* conveys as vividly as can be the atmosphere of a hot summer afternoon on the river at Asnières in the 1880's – more vividly even than the stories of Maupassant, in spite of their sparkle, because there is not in Seurat that touch of malice which almost always distorts the great writer's vision. With the *Grande-Jatte* we are carried a stage further. The observation is here detached, even amused, though it is hard for us to tell now whether or not Seurat realized and consciously stressed the comical outline of the bustles and the *art-nouveau* forms of the parasols. Here it is still a hot afternoon on the Seine, but the subject has been frozen into a sort of Egyptian frieze.

In *La Parade* the dream-like quality of the whole painting has grown stronger. The scene is still taken from ordinary life, but it is removed from it by the rigidity of the geometrical composition and by the extreme stylization of the actual hand-ling. But both in this painting and in *Le Chahut* the human element cannot be

5

disregarded; indeed in *Le Chahut* it is hard to believe that a point of satire was not intended.

Such considerations were however for Fry unimportant compared with the questions of formal harmony, in which Seurat's paintings are so pre-eminently successful, and although he observes them – and in his comments on *La Parade* observes them with humour – they are not for him an essential element in Seurat's greatness. Or rather – should one say? – they were not important for him at the time he wrote his two essays on this artist, for there is ample evidence to show that in his last years Fry was changing his approach towards painting and towards the basic principles of aesthetics. There are passages in his lecture on Rembrandt, recently published in *Apollo*, which show that he was once again concerned with the problem whether great illustration could be great art. In this case he still maintains, by implication, his old view, because he only admits Rembrandt to be a great painter in his last years, when, according to him, he had more or less ceased to be interested in 'illustration'. In his book on French painting, written on the occasion of the great exhibition at Burlington House in 1932, he seems to go further, and his analysis of the genre paintings of Chardin shows an understanding of the psychological subtleties of this artist that would make any 'traditional' critic jealous.

Within a very few years of his death in 1934 Fry's ideas were to be exposed to violent attack. Partly under the influence of Marxist aesthetics the younger generation were to react against his extreme statement of the 'pure form' doctrine; they felt – and not without reason – that Fry's view that the work of the great artist does not touch any of 'the finer issues of life' imposed a limitation on art which was not acceptable and that it left unexplained too many categories of works of art. It meant in effect dismissing as mere illustrators artists like Van Gogh in the near past, Rembrandt in the less remote past, and beyond that the whole art of the Middle Ages, as devoted to the service of religion instead of to the solving of purely plastic problems.

We were certainly violent in our reaction against Fry, but I have no doubt that, if he had still been alive, he would have enjoyed arguing with those who were attacking him; because, though he was a prophet, he never pontificated; he would always listen to the ideas of others, however young and however arrogant, and his own theories, which were certainly, so to speak, under review in his last years, might well have changed and have helped those younger than himself to arrive at a reasonable synthesis of their views and his own earlier ideas.

LONDON, 1965   ANTHONY BLUNT

GEORGES SEURAT

by Roger Fry

THE ACQUISITION by the Tate Gallery through the Courtauld Fund of Seurat's *Bathers* [Plate 15, now in the National Gallery], the purchase by an American for a high price of the *Grande-Jatte* [Plate 21, now in the Chicago Art Institute], the acquisition by the Louvre of *Le Cirque* [Plate 48], and lately an exhibition of his works at the Lefèvre Gallery [*Pictures and Drawings by Georges Seurat*, April - May 1926], all show that Seurat is at last coming into his inheritance. That he has not already done so long ago may at first sight seem surprising. It is due partly to the special character of Seurat's genius, partly to the accident that, just when he might have emerged, Cézanne, himself long overdue, occupied the field to the exclusion of every rival. But now that Cézanne's contribution has gradually been assimilated by the artistic consciousness of our day, it is evident that, if we set aside Renoir and Degas, whose work had long been accepted, the other outstanding figure of later nineteenth-century art is that of Seurat.

None the less he will, I think, always make rather a limited appeal. There was in his personality the strangest combination of an extreme sensibility and a devouring intellectual passion. He had, indeed, what is perhaps a good thing for an artist, more intellect than judgment. He had a passion for reducing the results of sensation to abstract statements, such, for instance, as his well-known formula of the effect of lines in composition, namely, that gaiety is given by lines ascending from the horizontal, calmness by horizontal lines, and sadness by descending lines. Gaiety, by the by, is about the last quality one would predicate of his *Cirque*, which is a deliberate demonstration of the effect of ascending lines. Such abstractions go but a very little way towards explaining the effect of so complex a thing as a pictorial design, still less can they be made much use of for the creation of such a complex. But it was a peculiarity of Seurat's intense love of method that it was by working along such lines as these that he was able, as it were, to lay by in pigeonholes those actual sensations upon which his sensibility was nourished. Thus he proceeded perpetually by analysis and classification working out separately and in turn the effective qualities of line, tone and colour. When he came to synthesize, the process almost appeared to him to be a mere logical deduction from the classified data of sensation – a deduction which could be stated by perfectly ascertained and preconceived methods. He is even said to have carried these so far that he was able to work all night in a feeble gaslight covering his huge canvases with his innumerable dots of colour, so exactly was the effect of each of the colours which he had previously mixed, ascertained.

Nothing can be imagined more deliberate, more pre-ordained than this method, nothing less like that divine afflatus of inspiration with which artists are often credited. And yet inspiration is the word one has to use before such strangely original conceptions as his landscapes declare. Who before Seurat ever conceived exactly the pictorial possibilities of empty space? Whoever before conceived that such vast areas of flat, unbroken surfaces as we see in his *Gravelines* could become the elements of a plastic design? And yet nothing less 'empty,' pictorially speaking, can be imagined. There is such a tense, imaginative conviction in these subtly-built-up statements of surface that one can well believe that Seurat's own definition of the art of painting, as 'the art of hollowing out a canvas', was so evident to him as to make the effort of the imagination in cutting away so much material proportional to the vastness and emptiness of the space thus excavated.

And this work is accomplished solely by reason of such a delicate sensibility that it can perceive and hold firm almost infinitesimal changes of value. It is by the accumulation of these almost invisible gradations that the result is obtained. That incredibly laborious technique of a minute pointillism was perhaps the only possible technique that would admit of such subtlety of variation. This, indeed, seems to me to have been of even greater importance to Seurat's aim than the extra luminosity claimed for it. It alone allowed of a sufficiently slow and tentative approach to the final statement, it alone made evident the slightest changes of tone. Often, indeed, the whole structure of a design is held together by those slight changes of tone which are due to illusion, as when one sees the sky just a little darker where it comes against the edge of a white sail or a building. And yet, for all this close adherence to observation, how unlike anything natural these pictures are! How utterly fixed and immovable everything is! His pictures are alive, indeed, but not with the life of nature. He will paint air and almost nothing but air filled with light, but there is no breath in his air. If his designs live and breathe it is by the tension of the imaginative concentration which they reveal and impel us to share. Seurat is of the lineage of Poussin, and he is as austerely aloof and detached as he.

Seurat's ambition was as vast as his disinterestedness was complete. He attacked and carried through with a kind of inspired and yet ant-like patience the most terrifying pictorial problems. To conciliate those fleeting evanescent atmospheric effects which the Impressionists had noted in their rapid and fluent manner with the exacting canons of classic composition and to realize this completely on a large scale by the slow accumulation on the canvas of myriads of minute dots of colour might have deterred any one but a fanatic. And indeed there must have been something of a fanatical devotion beneath the rigorous intellect and reserved manner of this strange young man.

It was in the *Bathers* that he made the first grand demonstration of his new ideas. The scene is laid on the banks of the Seine just outside Paris. In the hot summer afternoon boys recline or sit, naked or partly dressed, on the bank with cast-off clothes and boots scattered on the grass, whilst others are playing in the water. This scene, which for most people contains the hint of some kind of lyrical beauty, is seen by Seurat with an almost inhuman detachment. How natural it would seem to accentuate the beauty of the naked forms by choice of pose or of lighting! How easy to mitigate the banality of boots and trousers! But here everything is given with the same even, unrelenting unemphatic precision of statement. There is no bias whatsoever. The hot haze of the summer afternoon whitens the luminous sky, half veils the distant factories and bridge, and plays over the luminous bodies in the foreground, and no one could render this enveloping with a more exquisitely tremulous sensibility, a more penetrating observation or more unfailing consistency, than Seurat; but, none the less, every contour of the ungainly shirt tucked into the half-drawn-up trousers, or of the boots and socks, is rendered with the same unchanging attention. Yet the effect is neither of lyric beauty, nor of banal or ironic realism. Seurat's aim lies behind and deeper than all such attitudes to the scene. It would be hard to find any word uncoloured enough to describe the mood this evokes. It is like that which comes to us from some of Piero della Francesca's monumental and motionless groups. It is a mood of utter withdrawal from all the ordinary as well as all the poetic implications of things into a region of pure and almost abstract harmony. For that, indeed, is the secret of this great composition, the compelling harmony of all these forms, the so evident inevitability of all its correspondences and correlations. Boots and trousers lose their everyday banality when they are implicated in so close-woven a texture of formal harmony, however relentlessly their shapes are defined. One is forced even to rejoice that boots have tabs, so evidently do they here become the key to a whole sequence of rhythmic phrasing. And no less does the beauty and charm of the summer sunshine sink into the background of consciousness and become only another part of the colour organization. But yet, in spite of the exactitude and rigour of its harmony, this picture retains also something of its quality of im-mediacy, of a thing that was actually seen and seized on by the imagination in a single ecstatic moment. It is just that quality that Seurat's passionate research for abstract principles and scientific method might, one guesses, endanger. With him the balance between sensibility and doctrine was a delicate one. If the doctrine

9

were to cease to be amenable to constant correction by the sensibility it might become the predominant partner; demonstration would replace inspiration and theory passion. There was certainly a tendency for this to happen towards the end of Seurat's short life. That his sensibility would have regained the upper hand I do not doubt, but the balance sometimes inclines against it. The fact is that his method – he always called it '*ma méthode*', and any suggestion of infringement of his claim to have originated it moved him to something as near to self-assertiveness as his reserve and self-possession admitted – his method became increasingly his great passion, until he came to regard his pictures almost as demonstrations of its validity.

In the *Bathers* the method was not yet fully developed. The colour was put on in small dabs broken across by dabs of other colours, but those colours were always mixed on the palette to give the desired tint. He had not yet analysed the colours into more or less pure notes which should make up the required tint by means of optical mixture. Such a complete analysis implied, of course, much smaller units of colour, and this was finally attained by the juxtaposition of small round dots of the pure colours necessary to produce any required resultant.

The *Grande-Jatte* was the first application of the method in its amended and final form. It presents a world from which life and movement are banished, and all is fixed for ever in the rigid frame of its geometry. The *Poseuses* [now in the Barnes Collection, Merion, Pennsylvania. The small version now in the possession of Artemis, S.A., is reproduced in colour, Plate 38], which was the most important work of the Lefèvre exhibition, follows closely on that. It is not so ambitious, but even more than with that, one feels that it has never quite been 'seen'. The *Grande-Jatte* was created by assembling innumerable separate studies, an assembly in which everything took its place according to the principles of harmony which Seurat had elaborated. In the *Poseuses* the same method is employed. Seurat has made the same model pose in back, side and front views in a corner of his room, one side of which is completely filled by his painting of the Grande-Jatte. One feels that the poses have been found in order to fit a preconceived geometric scheme. Certainly the position of every single object and every part of the contour of every object has been ascertained to an almost incredible nicety. One cannot move a button or a ribbon without disaster to this amazingly complete and closely knit system. Since Poussin surely no one has been able to design in such elaborate and perfect counterpoint. But I come back to my feeling that here the harmony has been arrived at almost by trial and error, by a perpetual adjustment and readjustment. I do not mean, of course, that such arrangement and adjustment of one thing to another was the result of any merely intellectual calculation. It needed in order to succeed nothing less than Seurat's impeccable sense of proportion, of quantities, of tone and colour values, and his marvellous sense of balance of direction. What I mean is that, none the less, one feels that at no moment did the rhythmic idea flash into the artist's consciousness as a melody suggests itself to a musician. Still there it is, a wonderfully strange and original composition almost disquieting in its fixity. It is a very epitome of its author's theories of analogy. The analogies run through it even to the minutest details, analogies of form and analogies of colour. In colour, for instance, the violets, greens and reds of the Grande-Jatte find their analogies in the wall, the mounted drawings and the green garment or bag so carefully hung upon it, and in the bright rust reds of the sofa and parasol.

The main idea of the composition is of two long uprights, one, the central nude, the other the seated nude prolonged into the two upright figures of the Grande-Jatte. The picture is thus divided exactly into two equal halves, a bold application of Poussin's favourite practice. One half is occupied by the Grande-Jatte, the other by the nearly blank wall at right angles to it. This right-hand half has, instead of a third upright, a pyramid into which the seated figure is almost forcibly fitted. The original idea of the central standing nude is to be seen in a very beautiful drawing published in M. Coquiot's book.* It was standing firm with both legs together. But Seurat felt the need of an analogy, in the left-hand half of the picture, to the pyramid in the right, and has made the model's right leg stick out so as to be almost exactly parallel with the left-hand side of his pyramid, in order to do so. There can be no doubt to my mind that this was right from the point of view of the perfection of the composition, but it has led to a certain meagreness in the drawing of this figure. The volumes here seem wanting in fullness, especially as compared with the surprising beauty and ease of the nude to the left. Just with regard to this central figure something too literal, something of the unassimilated fact, seems to have persisted. It lacks the great style of most of Seurat's drawing.

It is for such reasons that I cannot share the widely expressed opinion of my fellow critics that this is a greater masterpiece than the *Bathers*. It no doubt represents a further stage in the development of Seurat's method, but it is too much put together, it has lost something of the conviction and immediacy which had not yet been subordinated to his science when he did the *Bathers*, and which still persists in the landscapes of the last period. I cannot doubt that if he had lived Seurat would have found a way to put his completed method at the service of his sensibility. What revelations his early death deprived us of!

Certainly *Les Poseuses* shows once more that strange aloofness of Seurat's spirit which we noted in the *Bathers*; but it is less remarkable here where the

* *Seurat* by G. Coquiot, Paris 1924, plate opposite p. 160.

deliberate arrangement by the artist of the models in the studio gives already a certain air of unreality to the thing seen. But the same characteristic of Seurat's attitude awakens an almost disquieting feeling before the later *Jeune Femme se poudrant*, which was shown by Mr. Paul Rosenberg recently in London [Plate 42, now at the Courtauld Institute Galleries]. This is, indeed, one of the strangest pictures I know, so utterly remote is the point of departure from the place to which Seurat carries us. It is as though he had made a bet that he would take the most intractable material possible and yet mould it to his ends. This impossible woman, in the grotesque *déshabillé* of the 'eighties, surrounded by every horror of gimcrack finery of the period, might have inspired Daumier to a grim satire, or Guys to an almost lyrical delight in its exuberance, or Degas to a bitter and merciless epigrammatic exposure, or Lautrec to an indulgently ironical scherzo; but Seurat passes over all such implications with an Olympian indifference, he treats the subject with religious solemnity and carries it into a region of abstract beauty. No Byzantine mosaic, however solemnly hieratic, could be more remote than this from all suggestion of 'La vie Parisienne'. The design is affirmed with an almost oppressive decision. We are forbidden to imagine the slightest tremor of change in these impeccable contours. By incessant revision the position of everything has been ascertained down to the minutest fraction. At first it seems to be all surface – contours revealed by spots of pure but elusive colour – and then these almost imperceptible changes of colour build up for us solid volumes bathed in a faint glowing light. There is scarcely any tone contrast, no definite light and shade, and yet in the end these volumes assert themselves with overpowering completeness. For all its decorative flatness, for all its theoretical and abstract colouring, this is intensely real, but for all its reality nothing of the original theme, of the thing seen, remains untransformed, all has been assimilated and remade by the idea. And perhaps this complete transmutation of the theme by the idea is the test of great art. It means that in proportion as a picture attains to this independent reality and inherent significance the element of illustration drops out altogether and becomes irrelevant.

Near by, in the French Gallery, there hung a large composition of Picasso's, representing a 'Mother and Child', to which he had given colossal proportions and a preternatural massiveness of limb. To a prolonged gaze these seemed to become but airy trifles beside the immutable fixity of Seurat's woman.

The landscapes seen at the Lefèvre Gallery all belong more or less to the period of complete pointillism, though in some cases Seurat's earlier method of small swept brush strokes persists underneath the fine network of dots. Each in its entirely distinct way is, to my mind, a complete and irrefutable discovery. They are all primarily designs of specially conceived spaces filled by specially interpreted luminosities and colour vibrations. How perfect Seurat's insight was into such appearances and how nice his control of expression, can be realized when we compare the opalescent pearly greys of the *Courbevoie* [Plate 29, now in the Courtauld Institute Galleries] with the flaming whiteness of the *Gravelines* [now in the collection of Lord Butler] and the dither of sunlight in *Le Port* [Plate 44, now at the John Herron Art Institute, Indianapolis]. But as beautiful and surprising as any is the *Port-en-Bessin* [now in the Museum of Modern Art, New York], where the shadows of still clouds hanging over the sunlit sea make an exquisite arabesque, picked up again by the patterns of the turf on the weathered down in the foreground. When viewed at a short range this appears as an almost flat pattern design, but retire to the other end of the room and the planes stretch to infinite distances, with almost the effect of an illusion.

It is one of the peculiarities of the pointillist method that tones which are so near together as to be indistinguishable close at hand become strongly contrasted when viewed from farther off. It is this that enabled Seurat to keep the surface of his canvas so unaccented and yet to produce an almost exaggerated salience and depth of relief. Several of these landscapes have fortunately retained their original frames, flat pieces of wood covered by the artist with his interminable spots of colour. Again, we see his mastery of effects of contrast and his exacting logic. The argument, one sees, must have gone somewhat thus : the function of a frame is to cut off the imagined picture space from the actual space of the room. To do this there should be an equal contrast between frame and picture at every point. But with a gilt frame the contrast cannot be equal at every point. It is strong where the gilt comes against a dark mass in the picture, weaker where it opposes a light, not to mention the even greater differences of colour contrast which this uniform gold implies. Seurat, therefore, set to work so to paint the frame as that, at each point, both colour and tone contrasts should be equal, and one cannot deny that he has succeeded to perfection. Hardly less remarkable is the fact that a precisely similar technique in frame and picture produces in one case a solid flatness, in the other the illusion of recession and distance.

Seurat's artistic personality was compounded of qualities which are usually supposed to be opposed and incompatible. On the one hand, his extreme and delicate sensibility, on the other a passion for logical abstraction and an almost mathematical precision of mind. On the one hand he accepted the whole body of Impressionist discovery about appearance even to the point of stating those phenomena which, even while we observe them, we know to be illusory, on the other hand, the mere statement of appearance which so preoccupied the Impressionists has no importance whatever for him. Appearance as revealed by Impressionist researches is nothing to him but the raw material out of which he builds, and his building is so purely logical and architectural, so precisely balanced and so nicely proportioned that the final result is utterly remote from appearance. The question of verisimilitude hardly occurs to one, so little can we refer his pictures to anything outside themselves, so completely does the created reality hold us by the laws of its self-contained system.

No doubt, at all times in the history of art we find that newly discovered data of appearance become the basis for new ventures in design with a consequent modification and extension of the esthetic sensibility. What is rare and what makes Seurat's genius so surprising is that in the few years of his activity he was able, starting entirely *de novo* with the large body of new data which Impressionism supplied, together with his own additional observations on irradiation and the physiological effects of contrast, to create out of that, altogether afresh and without any guiding tradition so extraordinarily complete an esthetic system, together with a new technical method so perfectly adapted to its expression.

[This essay appeared in 'The Dial', Camden, N.J., in September 1926]

ACKNOWLEDGEMENTS

The Publishers wish to thank private owners and public galleries for permission to reproduce the works in their collections. The publishers also wish to acknowledge with gratitude the permission given to them by Mrs Pamela Diamand and Messrs Chatto & Windus to reprint the essay on Seurat by Roger Fry.

LIST OF PLATES

31. IN HONFLEUR HARBOUR.
79,5×63 cm. 1886. Otterlo, Kröller-Müller Museum.

32. THE QUAY AT PORT-EN-BESSIN.
64,9×82,4 cm. 1888. Minneapolis, Institute of Arts.

33. SUNDAY AT PORT-EN-BESSIN.
66×82 cm. 1888. Otterlo, Kröller-Müller Museum.

34. THE EIFFEL TOWER.
24,1×15,2 cm. 1889. New York, Mr and Mrs Germain Seligman.

35. MODEL STANDING.
25,4×16,2 cm. 1886–1887. Paris, M. Georges Renand.

36. MODEL SEATED, PROFILE.
25×15,9 cm. 1886–1887. Paris, Louvre.

37. MODEL SEATED, BACK VIEW.
24,5×15,5 cm. 1886–1887. Paris, Louvre.

38. 'LES POSEUSES' (small version).
39,4×48,9 cm. 1888. Luxembourg, Artemis, S.A.

39–40. 'LA PARADE'.
99,7×150 cm. 1887–1888. New York, Metropolitan Museum of Art.

41. STUDY FOR 'LE CHAHUT'.
21,5×16,5 cm. 1889–1890. London, Courtauld Institute Galleries (Home House Trustees).

42. WOMAN POWDERING HERSELF.
94,5×79,2 cm. Probably 1889–1890. London, Courtauld Institute Galleries (Home House Trustees).

43. 'LE CHAHUT'.
169,1×139 cm. 1889–1890. Otterlo, Kröller-Müller Museum.

44. THE HARBOUR AT GRAVELINES.
73×92,7 cm. 1890. Indianapolis, The John Herron Art Institute.

45. THE HARBOUR AT GRAVELINES, EVENING.
65,3×82 cm. 1890. New York, Mr and Mrs W. A. M. Burden.

46. GRAVELINES.
15,9×24,8 cm. 1890. London, Courtauld Institute Galleries (Home House Trustees).

47. TREES AND BOATS.
15,9×25,4 cm. 1890. New York, Miss Alice Tully.

48. THE CIRCUS.
186×151,1 cm. 1890–1891. Paris, Louvre.

1. MAN LEANING ON A PARAPET. Between 1881 and 1883. Ridgefield, Connecticut, Mr. Albert Roothbert

2. THE STONE-BREAKER. 1882. Washington, D.C., Phillips Collection

3. IN THE FOREST AT PONTAUBERT. 1881 (?), reworked later. Saltwood Castle, Lord Clark

4. SUBURB. 1882. Troyes, M. Pierre Lévy

5. THE HORSE. About 1882. New York, Solomon R. Guggenheim Museum

6. HOUSES AT LE RAINCY. About 1882. Paris, Private Collection

7. THE WATERING-CAN. 1883. Upperville, Virginia, Mr. and Mrs. Paul Mellon

8. MAN PAINTING HIS BOAT. 1883. London, Lord Butler (Home House Trustees)

9. FIGURES IN A FIELD. About 1883. Private Collection

10. MAN FISHING FROM A MOORED BOAT. 1883. London, The Dowager Lady Aberconway

11. ANGLERS. 1883. Troyes, M. Pierre Lévy

12. HOUSE AMONG TREES. About 1883. Glasgow, City Art Gallery

13. HORSES IN THE RIVER. Study for 'Bathing at Asnières'. 1883–1884. London, The Dowager Lady Aberconway

14. BATHER SEATED. Study for 'Bathing at Asnières'. 1883–1884. Kansas City, The William Rockhill Nelson Gallery of Art

15. BATHING AT ASNIÈRES – 'UNE BAIGNADE'. 1883–1884, reworked about 1887. London, National Gallery

17. Detail of Plate 15

18. MAN FISHING. Study for 'Sunday Afternoon on the Ile de La Grande-Jatte'. 1884–1885. London, The Dowager Lady Aberconway

19. COUPLE WALKING. Study for 'Sunday Afternoon on the Ile de La Grande-Jatte'. 1884–1885. Tilton, Sussex, Lady Keynes

20. 'L'ILE DE LA GRANDE-JATTE'. 1884–1885. New York, Mr. John Hay Whitney

21. SUNDAY AFTERNOON ON THE ILE DE LA GRANDE-JATTE. 1883–1885, completed 1886. Chicago, Art Institute

22. Detail of Plate 21

23. THE RIVER SEINE AT COURBEVOIE. About 1885–1886. Paris, Private Collection

24. FIELD OF POPPIES. About 1884–1885. Maldon, Essex, Mrs. Pamela Diamand

25. 'LE BEC DU HOC, GRANDCAMP'. 1885. London, Tate Gallery

26. THE LIGHTHOUSE AT HONFLEUR. 1886. Formerly London, Sir A. Chester Beatty

27. THE BEACH AT BAS-BUTIN, HONFLEUR. 1886. Tournai, Musée des Beaux-Arts

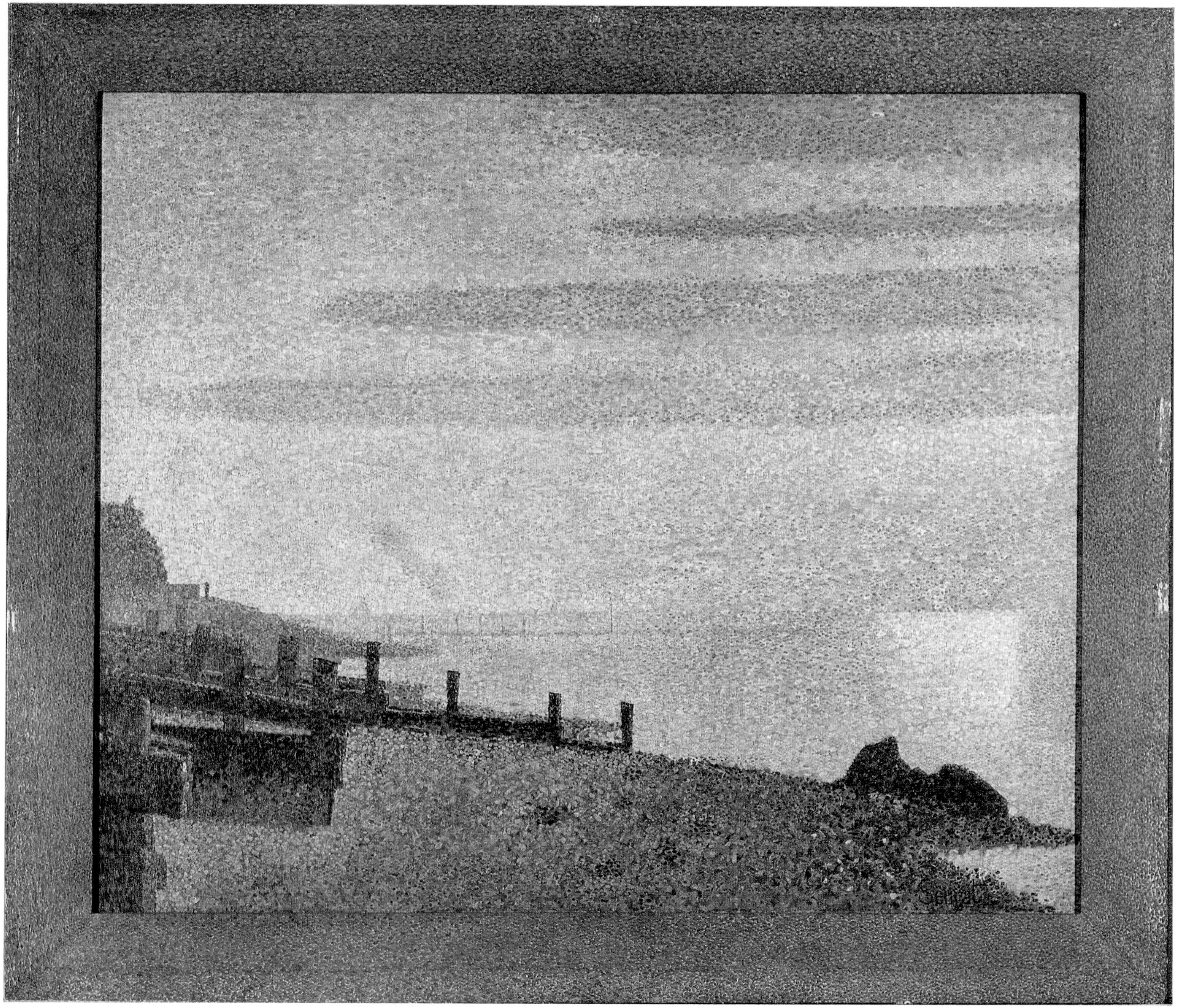

28. EVENING AT HONFLEUR. 1886. New York, Museum of Modern Art

30. 'LA MARIA', HONFLEUR. 1886. Prague, National Gallery

31. IN HONFLEUR HARBOUR. 1886. Otterlo, Kröller-Müller Museum

32. THE QUAY AT PORT-EN-BESSIN. 1888. Minneapolis, Institute of Arts

33. SUNDAY AT PORT-EN-BESSIN. 1888. Otterlo, Kröller-Müller Museum

34. THE EIFFEL TOWER. 1889. New York, Mr. and Mrs. Germain Seligman

35. MODEL STANDING. Study for 'Les Poseuses'. 1886–1887. Paris, M. Georges Renand

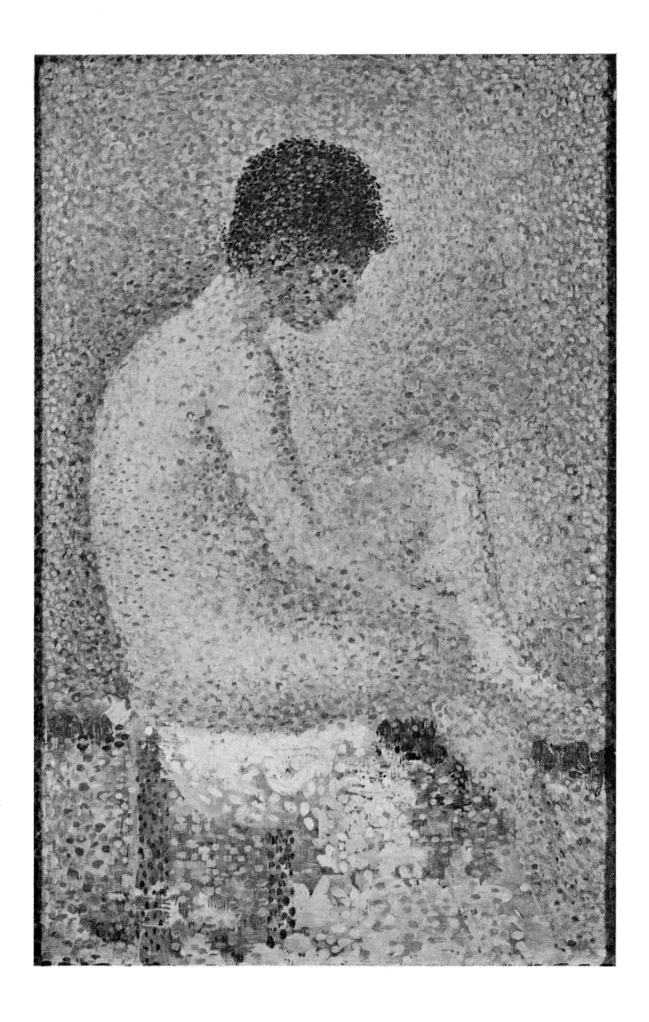

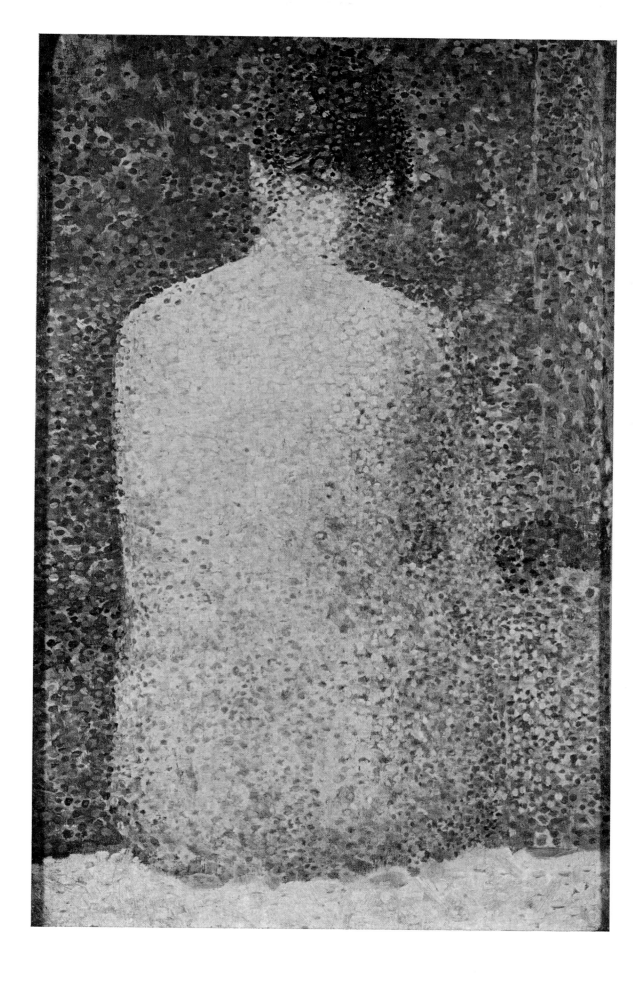

37. MODEL SEATED, BACK VIEW. Study for 'Les Poseuses'. 1886–1887. Paris, Louvre

38. 'LES POSEUSES' (small version). 1888. Luxembourg, Artemis S.A.

39. 'LA PARADE'. 1887–1888. New York, Metropolitan Museum of Art

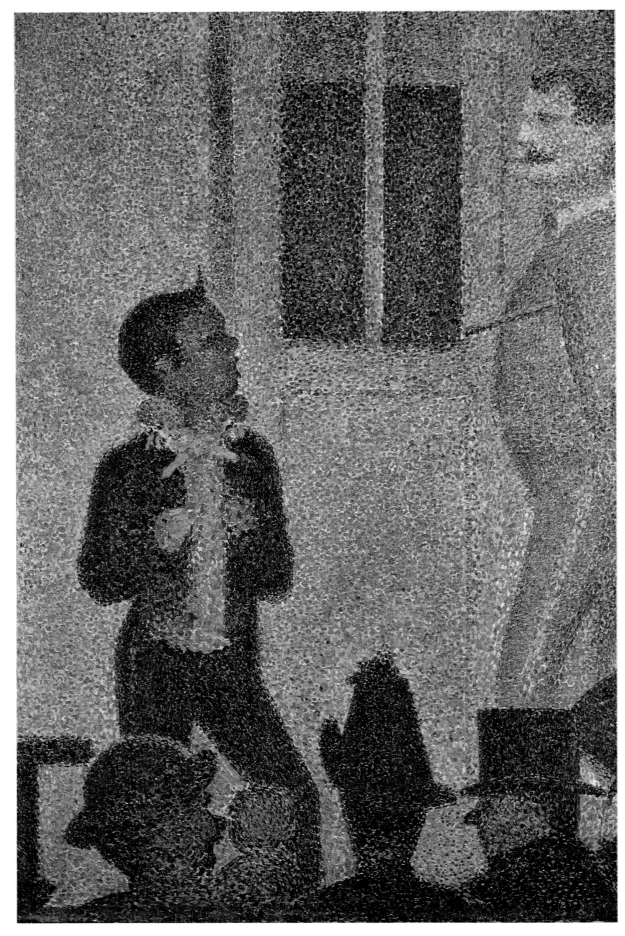

40. Detail of Plate 39

41. STUDY FOR 'LE CHAHUT'. 1889–1890. London, Courtauld Institute Galleries (Home House Trustees)

42. WOMAN POWDERING HERSELF. Probably 1889–1890. London, Courtauld Institute Galleries (Home House Trustees)

43. 'LE CHAHUT'. 1889–1890. Otterlo, Kröller-Müller Museum

44. THE HARBOUR AT GRAVELINES. 1890. Indianapolis, The John Herron Art Institute

45. THE HARBOUR AT GRAVELINES, EVENING. 1890. New York, Mr. and Mrs. A. M. Burden

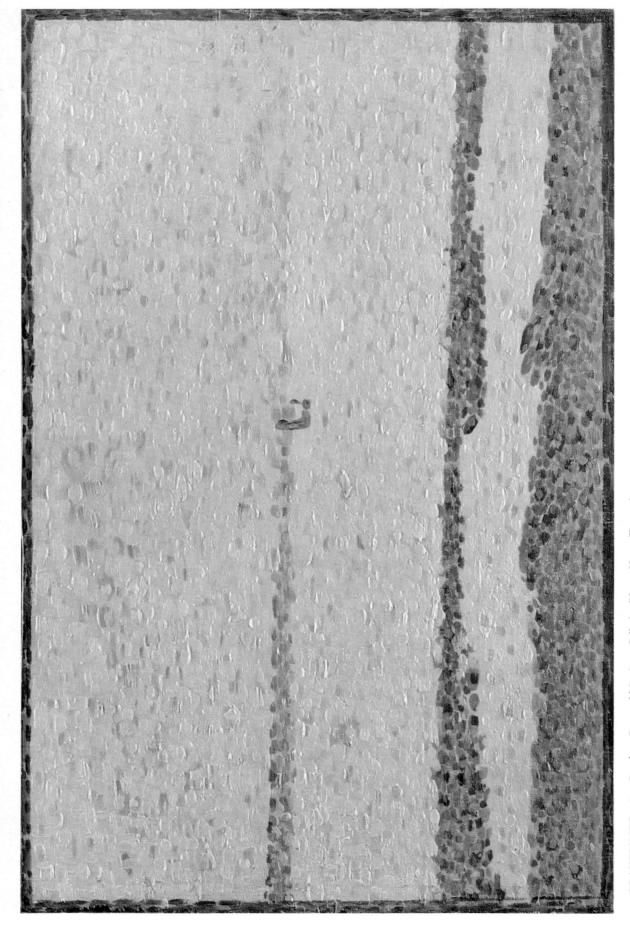

46. GRAVELINES. 1890. London, Courtauld Institute Galleries (Home House Trustees)

47. TREES AND BOATS. 1890. New York, Miss Alice Tully

48. THE CIRCUS. 1890–1891. Paris, Louvre